Cambridge University Library
Librarianship Series

PETER FOX

Reader instruction methods in academic libraries 1973

CAMBRIDGE
THE UNIVERSITY LIBRARY
1974

ML
2/5/21

REGULAR PUBLICATIONS FOR 1968-1969

133. John Courtenay, *A Poetical Review of the Literary and Moral Character of the Late Samuel Johnson* (1786). Introduction by Robert E. Kelley.

134. John Downes, *Roscius Anglicanus* (1708). Introduction by John Loftis.

135. Sir John Hill, *Hypochondriasis, a Practical Treatise on the Nature and Cure of that Disorder Call'd the Hyp or Hypo* (1766). Introduction by G. S. Rousseau.

136. Thomas Sheridan, *Discourse . . . Being Introductory to His Course of Lectures on Elocution and the English Language* (1759). Introduction by G. P. Mohrman.

137. Arthur Murphy, *The Englishman From Paris* (1756). Introduction by Simon Trefman. Previously unpublished manuscript.

138. [Catherine Trotter], *Olinda's Adventures* (1718). Introduction by Robert Adams Day.

SPECIAL PUBLICATION FOR 1968-1969

After THE TEMPEST. Introduction by George Robert Guffey.

Next in the continuing series of special publications by the Society will be *After THE TEMPEST*, a volume including the Dryden-Davenant version of *The Tempest* (1670); the "operatic" *Tempest* (1674); Thomas Duffet's *Mock-Tempest* (1675); and the "Garrick" *Tempest* (1756), with an Introduction by George Robert Guffey.

Already published in this series are:

1. John Ogilby, *The Fables of Aesop Paraphras'd in Verse* (1668), with an Introduction by Earl Miner.

2. John Gay, *Fables* (1727, 1738), with an Introduction by Vinton A. Dearing.

3. Elkanah Settle, *The Empress of Morocco* (1673) with five plates; *Notes and Observations on the Empress of Morocco* (1674) by John Dryden, John Crowne and Thomas Shadwell; *Notes and Observations on the Empress of Morocco Revised* (1674) by Elkanah Settle; and *The Empress of Morocco. A Farce* (1674) by Thomas Duffet; with an Introduction by Maximillian E. Novak.

Price to members of the Society, $2.50 for the first copy of each title, and $3.25 for additional copies. Price to non-members, $4.00. Standing orders for this continuing series of Special Publications will be accepted. British and European orders should be addressed to B. H. Blackwell, Broad Street, Oxford, England.

William Andrews Clark Memorial Library: University of California, Los Angeles

THE AUGUSTAN REPRINT SOCIETY

2520 CIMARRON STREET, LOS ANGELES, CALIFORNIA 90018

General Editors: William E. Conway, William Andrews Clark Memorial Library; George Robert Guffey, University of California, Los Angeles; Maximillian E. Novak, University of California, Los Angeles

Corresponding Secretary: Mrs. Edna C. Davis, William Andrews Clark Memorial Library

---

The Society's purpose is to publish rare Restoration and eighteenth-century works (usually as facsimile reproductions). All income of the Society is devoted to defraying costs of publication and mailing.

Correspondence concerning memberships in the United States and Canada should be addressed to the Corresponding Secretary at the William Andrews Clark Memorial Library, 2520 Cimarron Street, Los Angeles, California. Correspondence concerning editorial matters may be addressed to the General Editors at the same address. Manuscripts of introductions should conform to the recommendations of the MLA *Style Sheet*. The membership fee is $5.00 a year in the United States and Canada and £1.16.6 in Great Britain and Europe. British and European prospective members should address B. H. Blackwell, Broad Street, Oxford, England. Copies of back issues in print may be obtained from the Corresponding Secretary.

Publications of the first fifteen years of the Society (numbers 1–90) are available in paperbound units of six issues at $16.00 per unit, from the Kraus Reprint Company, 16 East 46th Street, New York, N.Y. 10017.

Make check or money order payable to THE REGENTS OF THE UNIVERSITY OF CALIFORNIA

1963-1964
104. Thomas D'Urfey, *Wonders in the Sun; or, The Kingdom of the Birds* (1706).

1964-1965
110. John Tutchin, *Selected Poems* (1685-1700).
111. Anonymous, *Political Justice* (1736).
112. Robert Dodsley, *An Essay on Fable* (1764).
113. T. R., *An Essay Concerning Critical and Curious Learning* (1698).
114. *Two Poems Against Pope:* Leonard Welsted, *One Epistle to Mr. A. Pope* (1730), and Anonymous, *The Blatant Beast* (1742).

1965-1966
115. Daniel Defoe and others, *Accounts of the Apparition of Mrs. Veal*.
116. Charles Macklin, *The Covent Garden Theatre* (1752).
117. Sir George L'Estrange, *Citt and Bumpkin* (1680).
118. Henry More, *Enthusiasmus Triumphatus* (1662).
119. Thomas Traherne, *Meditations on the Six Days of the Creation* (1717).
120. Bernard Mandeville, *Aesop Dress'd or a Collection of Fables* (1704).

1966-1967
123. Edmond Malone, *Cursory Observations on the Poems Attributed to Mr. Thomas Rowley* (1782).
124. Anonymous, *The Female Wits* (1704).
125. Anonymous, *The Scribleriad* (1742). Lord Hervey, *The Difference Between Verbal and Practical Virtue* (1742).
126. *Le Lutrin: an Heroick Poem, Written Originally in French by Monsieur Boileau: Made English by N. O.* (1682).

1967-1968
127-128. Charles Macklin, *A Will and No Will, or a Bone for the Lawyers* (1746). *The New Play Criticiz'd, or The Plague of Envy* (1747). Introduction by Jean B. Kern.
129. Lawrence Echard, Prefaces to *Terence's Comedies* (1694) and *Plautus's Comedies* (1694). Introduction by John Barnard.
130. Henry More, *Democritus Platonissans* (1646). Introduction by P. G. Stanwood.
131. John Evelyn, *The History of . . . Sabatai Sevi . . . The Suppos'd Messiah of the Jews* (1669). Introduction by Christopher W. Grose.
132. Walter Harte, *An Essay on Satire, Particularly on the Dunciad* (1730). Introduction by Thomas B. Gilmore.

Subsequent publications may be checked in the annual prospectus.

Publications of the first fifteen years of the Society (numbers 1—90) are available in paperbound units of six issues at $16.00 per unit, from the Kraus Reprint Company, 16 East 46th Street, New York, N.Y. 10017.

Publications in print are available at the regular membership rate of $5.00 yearly. Prices of single issues may be obtained upon request.

The Augustan Reprint Society

WILLIAM ANDREWS CLARK MEMORIAL LIBRARY

UNIVERSITY OF CALIFORNIA, LOS ANGELES

PUBLICATIONS IN PRINT

1948-1949
16. Henry Nevil Payne, *The Fatal Jealousie* (1673).
18. Anonymous, "Of Genius," in *The Occasional Paper*, Vol. III, No. 10 (1719), and Aaron Hill, Preface to *The Creation* (1720).

1949-1950
19. Susanna Centlivre, *The Busie Body* (1709).
20. Lewis Theobald, *Preface to the Works of Shakespeare* (1734).
22. Samuel Johnson, *The Vanity of Human Wishes* (1749), and two *Rambler* papers (1750).
23. John Dryden, *His Majesties Declaration Defended* (1681).

1951-1952
31. Thomas Gray, *An Elegy Wrote in a Country Churchyard* (1751), and *The Eton College Manuscript*.

1952-1953
41. Bernard Mandeville, *A Letter to Dion* (1732).

Who firmly scorn'd, when in a lowly state,
To flatter vice, or court the vain and great [51];
Whose heart still felt a sympathetick glow,
Prompt to relieve man's variegated woe;
Whose ardent hope, intensely fix'd on high,
Saw future bliss with intellectual eye.
Still in his breast Religion held her sway,
Disclosing visions of celestial day;
And gave his soul, amidst this world of strife,
The blest reversion of eternal life:
By this dispell'd, each doubt and horrour flies,
And calm at length in holy peace he dies.

   The sculptur'd trophy, and imperial bust,
That proudly rise around his hallow'd dust,
Shall mould'ring fall, by Time's slow hand decay'd,
But the bright meed of virtue ne'er shall fade.
Exulting Genius stamps his sacred name,
Enroll'd for ever in the dome of Fame.

[51] It is observable that Dr. Johnson did not prefix a dedication to any one of his various works.

THE END.

Though proudly fplenetick, yet idly vain,
Accepted flattery, and dealt difdain.—
E'en fhades like thefe, to brilliancy ally'd,
May comfort fools, and curb the Sage's pride.

Yet Learning's fons, who o'er his foibles mourn,
To lateft time fhall fondly view his urn;
And wond'ring praife, to human frailties blind,
Talents and virtues of the brighteft kind;
Revere the man, with various knowledge ftor'd,
Who fcience, arts, and life's whole fcheme explor'd;

confederated with *truth*, had fuch force as authority was unable to refift.— It was from the time when he firft began to patronize the Irifh, that they may date their riches, and profperity. He taught them firft to know their own intereft, their weight and their ftrength, and gave them fpirit to affert that *equality* with their fellow-fubjects to which they have been ever fince making vigorous advances, and to claim thofe *rights* which they have at laft eftablifhed."

The truth indeed feems to be, that Dr. Johnfon, though he had been bred in high-church principles, and always expreffed himfelf in controverfial argument like a Tory, poffeffed a high independent fpirit, and appears to have been a friend to the rights of man. His definition of the word *Caitiff*, in his Dictionary, may throw fome light on this part of his character. " Caitiff. [*cattivo*, Ital. a flave; whence it came to fignify a bad man, with fome implication of meannefs; as *knave* in Englifh, and *fur* in Latin; fo *certainly does flavery deftroy virtue.*

Ἥμισυ τῆς ἀρετῆς ἀποαινυῖαι δύλιον ἦμαρ.

A flave and a fcoundrel are fignified by the fame words in many languages.] A mean villain," &c. See alfo that animated paffage in his *London*, beginning, " Here let thofe reign," &c.

Who

Till gathering force, they more and more expand,
And with new virtue fertilise the land.

Thus sings the Muse, to Johnson's memory just,
And scatters praise and censure o'er his dust;
For through each checker'd scene a contrast ran,
Too sad a proof, how great, how weak is man!
Though o'er his passions conscience held the rein,
He shook at dismal phantoms of the brain:
A boundless faith that noble mind debas'd,
By piercing wit, energick reason grac'd:
A generous Briton [50], yet he seems to hope
For James's grandson, and for James's Pope:
With courtly zeal fair freedom's sons defames [51],
Yet, like a Hamden, pleads Ierne's claims [52].

Though

[50] When Dr. Johnson repeated to Mr. Boswell Goldsmith's beautiful eulogium on the English nation, his eyes filled with tears.—Boswell's *Tour*, p. 431.—See also the Dissertation on the Bravery of the English common Soldiers, at the end of the *Idler*.

[51] See *Taxation no Tyranny*.

[52] Though Dr. Johnson has called Hamden the *zealot of rebellion*, yet that distinguished patriot could not have expressed himself with more ardour in the cause of liberty, than Dr. Johnson does in the following passage in his Life of Swift: " In the succeeding reign [that of George I.] he delivered Ireland from plunder and *oppression*; and shewed that wit, confederated

Amid thefe names can Boswell be forgot,
Scarce by North Britons now efteem'd a Scot [49]?
Who to the fage devoted from his youth,
Imbib'd from him the facred love of truth;
The keen refearch, the exercife of mind,
And that beft art, the art to know mankind.—
Nor was his energy confin'd alone
To friends around his philofophick throne;
Its influence wide improv'd our letter'd ifle,
And lucid vigour mark'd the general ftyle:
As Nile's proud waves, fwol'n from their oozy bed,
Firft o'er the neighbouring meads majeftick fpread;

    There can be little doubt, confidering the antiquity and early civilifation of Hindoftan, that both the philofophy and beautiful mythology of the Greeks were drawn from that part of Afia.

    [49] The following obfervation in Mr. Bofwell's *Journal of a Tour to the Hebrides*, may fufficiently account for that gentleman's being " now fcarcely efteem'd a Scot" by many of his countrymen: " If he [Dr. Johnfon] was particularly prejudiced againft the Scots it was becaufe they were more in his way; becaufe he thought their fuccefs in England rather exceeded the due proportion of their real merit; and becaufe he could not but fee in them that nationality which, I believe, no liberal-minded Scotchman will deny." Mr. Bofwell indeed is fo free from national prejudices, that he might with equal propriety have been defcribed as—
    " Scarce by *South* Britons now efteem'd a Scot."

And you, Malone, to critick learning dear,
Correct and elegant, refin'd, though clear,
By studying him, acquir'd that classick taste,
Which high in Shakspeare's fane thy statue plac'd.
Near Johnson Steevens stands, on scenick ground,
Acute, laborious, fertile, and profound.
Ingenious Hawkesworth to this school we owe,
And scarce the pupil from the tutor know.
Here early parts accomplish'd Jones [47] sublimes,
And science blends with Asia's lofty rhimes:
Harmonious Jones! who in his splendid strains
Sings Camdeo's sports, on Agra's flowery plains;
In Hindu fictions while we fondly trace
Love and the Muses, deck'd with Attick grace [48].

Amid

[47] Sir William Jones produced that learned and ingenious work, *Poeseos Asiaticæ Commentarii*, at a very early age.

[48] " The Hindu God, to whom the following poem is addressed, appears evidently the same with the Grecian Eros, and the Roman Cupido.——His favourite place of resort is a large tract of country round Agra, and principally the plains of Matra, where Krishen also and the nine Gopia, who are clearly the Apollo and Muses of the Greeks, usually spend the night with musick and dance." Preface to the Hymn to Camdeo, translated from the Hindu language into Persian, and re-translated by Sir William Jones.

We *see* the Rambler with faſtidious ſmile
Mark the lone tree, and note the heath-clad iſle;
But when the heroick tale of Flora charms [44],
Deck'd in a kilt, he wields a chieftain's arms:
The tuneful piper ſounds a martial ſtrain,
And Samuel ſings, "The King ſhall have his ain":
Two Georges in his loyal zeal are ſlur'd [45],
A gracious penſion only ſaves the third!—
  By Nature's gifts ordain'd mankind to rule,
He, like a Titian, form'd his brilliant ſchool;
And taught congenial ſpirits to excel,
While from his lips impreſſive wiſdom fell.
Our boaſted GOLDSMITH felt the ſovereign ſway;
From him deriv'd the ſweet yet nervous lay.
To Fame's proud cliff he bade our Raphael riſe;
Hence REYNOLDS' pen with REYNOLDS' pencil vyes.
With Johnſon's flame melodious BURNEY glows [46],
While the grand ſtrain in ſmoother cadence flows.

    [44] The celebrated Flora Macdonald. See Boſwell's *Tour*.
    [45] See Note 4.
    [46] Dr. Burney's *Hiſtory of Muſick* is equally diſtinguiſhed by elegance and perſpicuity of ſtyle, and for ſcientifick knowledge.

Subtle when wrong, invincible when right,
Arm'd at all points, and glorying in his might,
Gladiator-like, he traverses the field,
And strength and skill compel the foe to yield.—
Yet have I seen him, with a milder air,
Encircled by the witty and the fair,
Ev'n in old age with placid mien rejoice
At beauty's smile, and beauty's flattering voice.—
With Reynolds' pencil, vivid, bold, and true,
So fervent Boswell gives him to our view.
In every trait we see his mind expand;
The master rises by the pupil's hand;
We love the writer, praise his happy vein,
Grac'd with the naiveté of the sage Montaigne.
Hence not alone are brighter parts display'd,
But ev'n the specks of character portray'd:

a good speech of interlocution, shews slowness; and a good reply or second speech, without a good settled speech, sheweth shallowness and weakness. As we see in beasts, that those that are weakest in the course, are yet *nimblest in the turn*; as it is betwixt the greyhound and the hare."—If this observation be just, Dr. Johnson is an exception to the rule; for he was certainly as *strong* " in the course, as nimble in the turn"; as ready in " reply," as in " a settled speech."

We

His mind exhaustless sped its vivid force,
Yet with unbated vigour held its course;
As some fix'd star fulfills heaven's great designs,
Lights other spheres, yet undiminish'd shines.

How few distinguish'd of the studious train
At the gay board their empire can maintain!
In their own books intomb'd their wisdom lies;
Too dull for talk, their slow conceptions rise:
Yet the mute author, of his writings proud,
For wit unshewn claims homage from the crowd;
As thread-bare misers, by mean avarice school'd,
Expect obeisance from their hidden gold.—
In converse quick, impetuous Johnson press'd
His weighty logick, or sarcastick jest:
Strong in the chace, and nimble in the turns [43],
For victory still his fervid spirit burns;
Subtle

he gave away, have bestowed fame, and probably fortune, on several persons. To the great disgrace of some of his clerical friends, forty sermons, which he himself tells us he wrote, have not yet been *deterré*.

[43] " A good continued speech (says Bacon in his Essays) without
a good

To guilt, to woe, the sacred debt was paid [41],
And helpless females bless'd his pious aid:
Snatch'd from disease, and want's abandon'd crew,
Despair and anguish from their victims flew;
Hope's soothing balm into their bosoms stole,
And tears of penitence restor'd the soul.
Nor did philanthrophy alone expand
His liberal heart, and ope his bounteous hand;
His *talents* ev'n he gave to friendship's claim [42],
And by the gift imparted wealth and fame:

His

[41] The dignified and affecting letter written by him to the King in the name of Doctor Dodd, after his condemnation, is justly, and, I believe, universally admired. His benevolence, indeed, was uniform and unbounded.——I have been assured, that he has often been so much affected by the sight of several unfortunate women, whom he has seen almost perishing in the streets, that he has taken them to his own house; had them attended with care and tenderness; and, on their recovery, clothed, and placed them in a way of life to earn their bread by honest industry.

[42] The papers in the ADVENTURER, signed with the letter T, are commonly attributed to one of Dr. Johnson's earliest and most intimate friends, Dr. Bathurst; but there is good reason to believe that they were written by Dr. Johnson, and given by him to his friend. At that time Dr. Johnson was himself engaged in writing the *Rambler*, and could ill afford to make a present of his labours. The various other pieces that

he

Johnson adventur'd boldly to transfuse
His vigorous sense into the Latian muse;
Aspir'd to shine by unreflected light,
And with a Roman's ardour *think* and write.
He felt the tuneful Nine his breast inspire,
And, like a master, wak'd the [39] soothing lyre:
Horatian strains a grateful heart proclaim,
While Sky's wild rocks resound his Thralia's name.—
Hesperia's plant, in some less skillful hands,
To bloom a while, factitious heat demands;
Though glowing Maro a faint warmth supplies,
The sickly blossom in the hot-house dies:
By Johnson's genial culture, art, and toil,
Its root strikes deep, and owns the fost'ring soil;
Imbibes our sun through all its swelling veins,
And grows a native of Britannia's plains.
  Soft-ey'd compassion, with a look benign
His fervent vows he offer'd at thy shrine;

[40] " Inter *ignotæ* strepitus *loquelæ*."—Ode to Mrs. Thrale.

Sublime as Juvenal, he pours his lays [37],
And with the Roman shares congenial praise:—
In glowing numbers now he fires the age,
And Shakspeare's sun relumes the clouded stage [38].

So full his mind with images was fraught,
The rapid strains scarce claim'd a second thought;
And with like ease his vivid lines assume
The garb and dignity of ancient Rome.—
Let college *versemen* trite conceits express,
Trick'd out in splendid shreds of Virgil's dress;
From playful Ovid cull the tinsel phrase,
And vapid notions hitch in pilfer'd lays;
Then with mosaick art the piece combine,
And boast the glitter of each dulcet line:

[37] *London*, a Satire, and *The Vanity of Human Wishes*, are both imitations of Juvenal. On the publication of *London* in 1738, Mr. Pope was so much struck by it, that he desired Mr. Dodsley, his bookseller, to find out the author. Dodsley having sought him in vain for some time, Mr. Pope said, he would very soon be *deterré*. Afterwards Mr. Richardson the painter found out Mr. Johnson, and Mr. Pope recommended him to Lord Gower.

[38] See the Prologue spoken by Mr. Garrick in 1747, on the opening of Drury-Lane theatre.

Johnson

Though metaphyficks fpread the gloom of night,
By reafon's ftar he guides our aching fight;
The bounds of knowledge marks; and points the way
To pathlefs waftes, where wilder'd fages ftray;
Where, like a farthing linkboy, Jennings ftands,
And the dim torch drops from his feeble hands.

Impreffive truth, in fplendid fiction dreft [35],
Checks the vain wifh, and calms the troubled breaft;
O'er the dark mind a light celeftial throws,
And fooths the angry paffions to repofe;
As oil effus'd illumes and fmooths the deep [36],
When round the bark the foaming furges fweep.—

But hark, he fings! the ftrain ev'n Pope admires;
Indignant Virtue her own bard infpires;

---

[35] See that fublime and beautiful Tale, *The Prince of Abyffinia*; and *The Rambler*, No. 65, 204, &c. &c.

[36] " The world is difpofed to call this a difcovery of Dr. Franklin's, (from his paper inferted in the Philofophical Tranfactions) but in this they are much miftaken. Pliny, Plutarch, and other naturalifts were acquainted with it.—" Ea natura eft olei, ut lucem afferat, ac tranquillar omnia, etiam mare, quo non aliud elementum implacabilius."
Memoirs of the Society of Manchefter.

In judgment keen, he acts the critick's part,
By reason proves the feelings of the heart;
In thought profound, in nature's study wise,
Shews from what source our fine sensations rise;
With truth, precision, fancy's claims defines,
And throws new splendour o'er the poet's lines [31].

When specious sophists with presumption scan
The source of evil, hidden still from man [32];
Revive Arabian tales [33], and vainly hope
To rival St. John, and his scholar, Pope [34];

In the Prologue on opening Drury-Lane theatre, he changed but one word, and that in compliment to Mr. Garrick. Some of his *Ramblers* were written while the printer's messenger was waiting to carry the copy to the press. Many of the *Idlers* were written at Oxford; Dr. Johnson often began his task only just in time not to miss the post, and sent away the paper without reading it over.

[31] See his admirable *Lives of the Poets,* and particularly his Disquisition on metaphysical and religious poetry.

[32] See his Review of Soame Jennings's *Essay on the Origin of Evil*; a masterpiece of composition, both for vigour of style and precision of ideas.

[33] Pope's or rather Bolingbroke's system was borrowed from the Arabian metaphysicians.

[34] The scheme of the *Essay on Man* was given by Lord Bolingbroke to Pope.

Though

To shed a radiance o'er his moral page,
And spread truth's sacred light to many an age?
For all his works with innate lustre shine,
Strength all his own, and energy divine.

While through life's maze he sent a piercing view,
His mind expansive to the object grew.
With various stores of erudition fraught,
The lively image, the deep-searching thought,
Slept in repose;—but when the moment press'd,
The bright ideas stood at once confess'd [30];
Instant his genius sped its vigorous rays,
And o'er the letter'd world diffus'd a blaze:
As womb'd with fire the cloud electrick flies,
And calmly o'er the horizon seems to rise;
Touch'd by the pointed steel, the lightning flows,
And all the expanse with rich effulgence glows.

In

---

[30] Dr. Johnson's extraordinary facility of composition is well known from many circumstances. He wrote forty pages of the Life of Savage in one night. He composed seventy lines of his Imitation of the Tenth Satire of Juvenal, and wrote them down from memory, without altering a word.

When no diverfity we trace between
The lofty moralift and gay fifteen²⁹.—
Yet genius ftill breaks through the encumbering phrafe;
His tafte we cenfure, but the work we praife:
There learning beams with fancy's brilliant dyes,
Vivid as lights that gild the northern fkies;
Man's complex heart he bares to open day,
Clear as the prifm unfolds the blended ray:
The picture from his mind affumes its hue;
The fhades too dark, but the defign ftill true.

 Though Johnfon's merits thus I freely fcan,
And paint the foibles of this wond'rous man;
Yet can I coolly read, and not admire,
When Learning, Wit and Poetry confpire

---

[29] See Victoria's Letter, Rambler, No. 130.—" I was never permitted to fleep till I had paffed through the cofmetick difcipline, part of which was a regular luftration performed with bean-flower water and may-dews; my hair was perfumed with a variety of unguents, by fome of which it was to be thickened, and by others to be curled. The foftnefs of my hands was fecured by medicated gloves, and my bofom rubbed with a pomade prepared by my mother, of virtue to difcufs pimples, and clear difcolorations."

To

In solemn pomp, with pedantry combin'd,
He vents the morbid sadness of his mind [26];
In scientifick phrase affects to smile,
Form'd on Brown's turgid Latin-English style [27]:
Too oft the abstract decorates his prose [28],
While measur'd ternaries the periods close:
But all propriety his Ramblers mock,
When Betty prates from Newton and from Locke;

[26] "In times and regions so disjoined from each other, that there can scarcely be imagined any communication of sentiments, either by commerce or tradition, has prevailed a general and uniform expectation of propitiating GOD by corporal austerities, of anticipating his vengeance by voluntary inflictions, and appeasing his justice by a speedy and cheerful submission to a less penalty when a greater is incurred."
Rambler, No. 110.

[27] The style of the *Ramblers* seem to have been formed on that of Sir Thomas Brown's *Vulgar Errors* and *Christian Morals*.
"But ice is water congealed by the frigidity of the air, whereby it acquireth no new form, but rather a consistence or determination of its defluency, and amitteth not its essence, but condition of fluidity. Neither doth there any thing properly conglaciate but water, or watery humidity, for the determination of quicksilver is properly fixation, that of milk coagulation, and that of oil and unctuous bodies only incrassation."—Is this written by Brown or Johnson?

[28] In the *Ramblers* the abstract too often occurs instead of the concrete;—one of Dr. Johnson's peculiarities.

When

The bulky tome his curious care refines,
Till the great work in full perfection shines:
His wide research and patient skill displays
What scarce was sketch'd in ANNA's golden days [24];
What only learning's aggregated toil
Slowly accomplish'd in each foreign soil [25].
Yet to the mine though the rich coin he trace,
No current marks his early essays grace;
For in each page we find a massy store
Of English bullion mix'd with Latian ore:

" In this work, when it shall be found that much is omitted, let it not be forgotten that much likewise is performed; and though no book was ever spared out of tenderness to the authour, and the world is little solicitous to know whence proceeded the faults of that which it condemns, yet it may gratify curiosity to inform it, that the ENGLISH DICTIONARY was written with *little assistance of the learned, and without any patronage of the great; not in the soft obscurities of retirement, or under the shelter of academick bowers, but amidst inconvenience and distraction, in sickness and in sorrow.*" Preface to Dr. Johnson's Dictionary.

[24] See Swift's letter to Lord Oxford for the institution of an academy to improve and fix the English language.

[25] The great French and Italian Dictionaries were not the productions of an individual, but were compiled by a body of Academicians in each country.

But who to blaze his frailties feels delight,
When the great author rises to our sight?
When the pure tenour of his life we view,
Himself the bright exemplar that he drew?
Whose works console the good, instruct the wise,
And teach the soul to claim her kindred skies.

By grateful bards his name be ever sung,
Whose sterling touch has fix'd the English tongue!
Fortune's dire weight, the patron's cold disdain,
" Shook off, as dew-drops from the lion's mane²²;"
Unknown, unaided, in a friendless state²³,
Without one smile of favour from the great;

The

---

²² " The incumbrances of fortune were shaken from his mind as *dew-drops from the lion's mane.*" Johnson's *Preface to his edition of Shakspeare.*

²³ Every reader of sensibility must be strongly affected by the following pathetick passages:—" Much of my life has been lost under the pressures of disease; much has been trifled away; and much has always been spent in provision for the day that was passing over me; but I shall not think my employment useless or ignoble, if by my assistance foreign nations and distant ages gain access to the propagators of knowledge, and understand the teachers of truth; if my labours afford light to the repositories of science, and add celebrity to Bacon, to Hooker, to Milton, and to Boyle."

[10]

Or when Moll Tofts, by throes parturient vext,
Saw her young rabbets peep from Efdras' text [21] !
To him such signs, prepar'd by myftick grace,
Had shewn the impending doom of Adam's race.

the former; &c.) be not an allegorical reprefentation of this comet, which returns once after five centuries, and goes down to the fun, and is there vehemently heated, and its outward regions diffolved; yet that it flies off again, and carries away what remains after that terrible burning; &c. and whether the *conflagration* and renovation of things, which fome fuch comet may bring on the earth, be not hereby prefigured, I will not here be pofitive: but I own, that I do not know of any folution of this famous piece of mythology and hieroglyphics, as this feems to be, that can be compared with it." *Ibid.* p. 196.

[21] " 'Tis here foretold [by Efdras] that there fhould be *figns in the woman*; and before all others this prediction has been verified in the famous *rabbet-woman of Surrey*, in the days of King George I.—This ftory has been fo unjuftly laughed out of countenance, that I muft diftinctly give my reafons for believing it to be true, and alleging it here as the fulfilling of this ancient prophecy before us.—1ft. The man-midwife, Mr. Howard of Godalmin in Surrey, a perfon of very great honefty, fkill and reputation in his profeffion, attefted it.—It was believed by King George to be real; and it was alfo believed by my old friends the Speaker and Mr. Samuel Collet, as they told me themfelves, and was generally by fober perfons in the neighbourhood. Nay Mr. Molyneux, the Prince's Secretary, a very inquifitive perfon, and my very worthy friend, affured me he had at firft fo great a diffidence in the truth of the fact, and was fo little biaffed by the other believers, even by the King himfelf, that he would not be fatisfied till he was permitted both to fee and feel the rabbet, *in that very paffage, whence we all come into this world.*"
Whifton's *Memoirs*, vol. ii. p. 110.

But

Religious Johnson, future life to gain,
Would ev'n submit to everlasting pain:
How clear, how strong, such kindred colours paint
The Roman epicure and Christian saint!
O, had he liv'd in more enlighten'd times,
When signs from heaven proclaim'd vile mortals' crimes,
How had he groan'd, with sacred horrors pale,
When Noah's comet shook her angry tail [19];
That wicked comet, which Will Whiston swore
Would burn the earth that she had drown'd before [20]!

Or

Dr. Johnson, in his last illness, is said to have declared (in the presence of Doctors H. and B.) that he would prefer a state of existence in eternal pain to annihilation.

[19] "This last comet (which appeared in the year 1680) I may well call the most remarkable one that ever appeared; since, besides the former consideration, I shall presently shew, that it is no other than that very comet, which came by the earth at the time of Noah's deluge, and *which was the cause of the same.*" Whiston's *Theory of the Earth*, p. 188.

[20] "Since 575 years appear to be the period of the comet that caused the deluge, what a learned friend who was the occasion of my examination of this matter, suggests, will deserve to be considered; viz. Whether the story of the phœnix, that celebrated emblem of the resurrection in Christian antiquity, (that it returns once after five centuries, and goes to the altar and city of the sun, and is there burnt; and another arises out of its ashes, and carries away the remains of

To recent wonders may deny his aid [17],
Nor own a busy zealot of the trade.

A coward wish, long stigmatiz'd by fame,
Devotes Mæcenas to eternal shame [18];

Religious

[7] From the following letter there is reason to apprehend that Dr. Adams would not support Mr. S——n, if he should add this to the other singular anecdotes that he has published relative to Dr. Johnson.

Mr. Urban, Oxford, Oct. 22d, 1785.

In your last month's Review of books, you have asserted, that the publication of Dr. Johnson's *Prayers* and *Meditations* appears to have been at the instance of Dr. Adams, Master of Pembroke College, Oxford. This, I think, is more than you are warranted by the editor's preface to say; and is so far from being true, that Dr. Adams never saw a line of these compositions, before they appeared in print, nor ever heard from Dr. Johnson, or the editor, that any such existed. Had he been consulted about the publication, he would certainly have given his voice against it: and he therefore hopes, that you will clear him, in as publick a manner as you can, from being any way accessary to it.

Wm. Adams.

> " Debilem facite manu,
> " Debilem pede, coxa;
> " Tuber adstrue gibberum;
> " Lubricos quate dentes;
> " Vita dum superest, bene est:
> " Hanc mihi, vel acuta
> " Si sedeam cruce, sustine." SENEC. EPIST. 101.

Let me but live, the fam'd Mæcenas cries,
Lame of both hands, and lame in feet and thighs;
Hump-back'd, and toothless;—all convuls'd with pain,
Ev'n on the cross,—so precious life remain.

Dr.

He sleeps and fasts[11], pens on himself a libel[12],
And still believes, but never reads the Bible[13].
Fame says, at school, of scripture science vain,
Bel and the Dragon smote him on the brain[14];
Scar'd with the blow, he shun'd the Jewish law,
And eyed the Ark with reverential awe[15]:
Let priestly S—h—n in a godly fit
The tale relate, in aid of Holy Writ;
Though candid Adams, by whom DAVID fell[16],
Who ancient miracles sustain'd so well,

[11] " I fasted, though less rigorously than at other times. I by negligence poured some milk into my tea. *Ibid.* p. 146.—Yesterday, I fasted, as I have always, or commonly done, since the death of Tetty; the fast was more painful than usual."

[12] " PURPOSES.

" To keep a journal. To begin this day. (Sept. 18th, 1766.)
" To spend four hours in study every day, and as much more as I can.
" To read a portion of Scripture in Greek every Sunday.
" To rise at eight.—Oct. 3d. Of all this I have done nothing." *Ibid.*

[13] " I resolved last Easter to read, within the year, the whole Bible; a great part of which I had never looked upon." *Meditations.*

[14] " I have never yet read the Apocrypha. When I was a boy I have read or heard Bel and the Dragon." *Meditations.*

[15] See the First Book of Samuel, ch. v. and vi. in which an account is given of the punishment of the Philistines for looking into the ark.

[16] The Rev. Dr. Adams of Oxford, distinguished for his answer to David Hume's *Essay on Miracles*.

To

On Scotland's kirk he vents a bigot's gall [7],
Though her young chieftains prophecy like SAUL [8]!
On Tetty's state his frighted fancy runs [9],
And Heaven's appeas'd by crofs unbutter'd buns [10]:

—But Archbishop Tillotson and Mr. Locke reason more philosophically, by asserting that " no doctrine, however clearly expressed in Scripture, is to be admitted, if it contradict the evidence of our senses:—For our evidence for the truth of revealed religion is *less* than the evidence for the truth of our senses, because, *even* in the first authors of our religion, it was no greater; and it is evident it must diminish in passing from them to us, through the medium of human testimony."—This question, however, may perhaps be better elucidated by the following Anecdote, preserved by Mr. Richardson, than by a more serious discussion:

" Mr. Pope, who loved to talk of Titcum, (one who used to be of the party with him, Gay, Swift, Craggs, and Addison, and that set, in his youth,) told us, that Gay went to see him as he was dying, and asked him, if he would have a priest; (for he was a papist,) ' No, said he, what should I do with them? But I would rather have one of them, than one of yours, of the two. Our fools, (continued he) write great books to prove that *bread* is *God*; but your booby (he meant Tillotson) has wrote a long argument to prove that *bread* is *bread*.' *Richardsoniana*, p. 167.

[7] See his conversation with Lord Auchinleck. Boswell's *Tour*.

[8] See the First Book of Samuel, ch. x.

[9] " And I commend to thy fatherly goodness the soul of my departed wife, beseeching thee to grant her whatever is best in her present state."
Johnson's *Meditations*.

[10] " I returned home, but could not settle my mind. At last I read a chapter. Then went down about six or seven, and eat two *crofs-buns*."
Meditations, p. 154.

He

At great Naſſau deſpiteful rancour flings [4],
But penſion'd kneels ev'n to uſurping kings:
Rich, old and dying, bows his laurel'd head,
And almoſt deigns to aſk ſuperfluous bread [5]."

A ſceptick once, he taught the letter'd throng
To doubt the exiſtence of fam'd Oſſian's ſong;
Yet by the eye of faith, in reaſon's ſpite,
Saw ghoſts and witches, preach'd up *ſecond ſight:*
For o'er his ſoul ſad Superſtition threw
Her gloom, and ting'd his genius with her hue.
On popiſh ground he takes his high church ſtation,
To found myſterious tenets through the nation [6];

On

---

[4] *Johnſon.* " I would tell truth of the two Georges, or of that ſcoundrel, King William. Boſwell's *Tour to the Hebrides,* p. 312.

[5] See his letter to Lord Thurlow, in which he ſeems to approve of the application (though he was not previouſly conſulted), thanks his Lordſhip for having made it, and even expreſſes ſome degree of ſurprize and reſentment on the propoſed addition to his penſion being refuſed.

[6] " If (added Dr. Johnſon) GOD had never ſpoken figuratively, we might hold that he ſpeaks literally, when he ſays, " This is my body." Boſwell's *Tour,* p. 67.—Here his only objection to tranſubſtantiation ſeems to reſt on the ſtyle of the Scripture being figurative elſewhere as well as in this paſſage. Hence we may infer, that he would otherwiſe have believed in it.

—But

With poignant taunt mild Shenstone's life arraigns,
His taste contemns, and sweetly-flowing strains;
At zealous Milton aims his tory dart,
But in his Savage finds a moral heart;

is well known, that he affected simplicity, and studiously avoided any display of learning, except where the subject made it absolutely necessary. Temporary, local, and political topicks compose too great a part of his works; but in a treatise that admitted " more thinking, more knowledge," &c. he naturally exerted all his powers.—Let us hear the author himself on this point.

" The greatest part of that book was finished above thirteen years since, (1696) which is eight years before it was published. The author was then young, his invention at the height, and his reading fresh in his head." And again: " Men should be more cautious in losing their time, if they did but consider, that to answer a book effectually requireth more pains and skill, more wit, learning and judgement, than were employed in writing it.---And the author assureth those gentlemen, who have given themselves that trouble with him, that his discourse is the product of the study, the observation, and the invention of *several years*; that he often blotted out more than he left; and if his papers had not been a long time out of his possession, they must still have undergone more severe corrections." *An Apology for the Tale of a Tub.*—With respect to this work being the production of Swift, see his letter to the printer, Mr. Benjamin Tooke, dated Dublin, June 29, 1710, and Tooke's Answer on the publication of *the Apology* and a new edition of the *Tale of a Tub.* Hawkesworth's edition of Swift's Works, 8vo. vol. xvi. p. 145.

Doctor Hawkesworth mentions, in his preface, that the edition of *A Tale of a Tub,* printed in 1710, was revised and corrected by the Dean a short time before his understanding was impaired, and that the corrected copy was, in the year 1760, in the hands of his kinsman, Mr. Deane Swift.

At

By subtle doubts would Swift's fair fame invade,
And round his brows the ray of glory shade [3];

With

[3] "He seemed to me to have an unaccountable prejudice against Swift. —He said to-day,—I doubt if the *Tale of a Tub* was his; it has so much more thinking, more knowledge, more power, more colour, than any of the works that are indisputably his. If it was his, I shall only say, he was *impar sibi*." Boswell's *Tour to the Hebrides*, p. 38.

Doctor Johnson's "unaccountable prejudice against Swift" may probably be derived from the same source as Blackmore's, if we may venture to form a judgement from the panegyrick he bestows on the following groundless invective, expressly aimed at Swift as the author of *A Tale of a Tub*, which he quotes in his life of Blackmore: "Several, in their books, have many sarcastical and spiteful strokes at religion in general; while others make themselves pleasant with the principles of the Christian. Of the last kind, this age has seen a most audacious example, in the book intituled "*A Tale of a Tub*." Had this writing been published in a pagan or *popish* nation, who are *justly* impatient of all indignity offered to the established religion of their country, no doubt but the author would have received the punishment he deserved.---But the fate of this impious buffoon is very different; for in a protestant kingdom, zealous of ther civil and religious immunities, he has not only escaped affronts and the effects of publick resentment, but has been caressed and patronised by persons of great figure of all denominations."

The malevolent dullness of bigotry alone could have inspired Blackmore with these sentiments. The fact is, that the *Tale of a Tub* is a continued panegyrick on the Church of England, and a bitter satire on Popery, Calvinism, and every sect of dissenters. At the same time I am persuaded, that every reader of taste and discernment will perceive in many parts of Swift's other writings strong internal proofs of that style which characterises the *Tale of a Tub*; especially in the *Publick Spirit of the Whigs*. It

is

[2]

A paſsport grants to Pomfret's diſmal chimes,
To Yalden's hymns, and Watts's holy rhimes [2];

[2] "The Poems of Dr. Watts were by my recommendation inſerted in this collection; the readers of which are to impute to me whatever pleaſure or wearineſs they may find in the peruſal of Blackmore, Watts, Pomfret and Yalden." Johnſon's *Life of Watts.*

The following ſpecimen of their productions may be ſufficient to enable the reader to judge of their reſpective merits:

"Alas, Jeruſalem! alas! where's now
  "Thy priſtine glory, thy unmatch'd renown,
"To which the heathen monarchies did bow?
  "Ah, hapleſs, miſerable town!."

Eleazar's *Lamentation over Jeruſalem,*
paraphraſed by Pomfret.

"Before the Almighty Artiſt fram'd the ſky,
"Or gave the earth its harmony,
"His firſt command was for thy light;
"He view'd the lovely birth, and bleſſed it:
"*In purple ſwaddling bands it ſtruggling lay,*
"Old Chaos then a chearful ſmile put on,
"And from thy beauteous form did firſt preſage its own."

Yalden's *Hymn to Light.*

"My chearful ſoul now all the day
  "Sits waiting here and ſings;
"Looks through the ruins of her clay,
  "And practiſes her wings.
"O, rather let this fleſh decay,
  "The ruins wider grow!
"Till glad to ſee the enlarged way,
  "I ſtretch my pinions through."

A Sight of Heaven in Sickneſs, by Iſaac Watts.

By

A

POETICAL REVIEW, &c.

A Generous tear will Caledonia shed?
　Her ancient foe, illustrious Johnson's dead;
Mac-Ossian's sons may now securely rest,
Safe from the bitter sneer, the cynick jest[1].
The song of triumph now I seem to hear,
And these the sounds that vibrate on my ear:
" Low lies the man, who scarce deigns Gray to praise,
But from the tomb calls Blackmore's sleeping lays;

---

[1] " A Scotchman must be a sturdy moralist, who does not prefer Scotland to truth." Johnson's *Journey to the Western Isles of Scotland.*

A POETICAL REVIEW

OF THE

LITERARY AND MORAL CHARACTER

OF THE LATE

SAMUEL JOHNSON, L.L.D.

WITH NOTES.

By JOHN COURTENAY, Esq.

THE THIRD EDITION, CORRECTED.

Man is thy theme; his virtue, or his rage,
Drawn to the life, in each elaborate page. WALLER.

———*immensæ veluti connexa carinæ*
Cymba minor. STATIUS.

LONDON:
PRINTED FOR CHARLES DILLY IN THE POULTRY.
M DCC LXXXVI.

BIBLIOGRAPHICAL NOTE

The text of this edition of *A Poetical Review of the Literary and Moral Character of the Late Samuel Johnson, L.L.D., with Notes* is reproduced from a copy in the Beinecke Rare Book and Manuscript Library, Yale University.

9. *Letters*, II, 428, 425. Boswell tried to negotiate loans for Courtenay, and made a successful application to Reynolds. See *Private Papers*, XVII, 85-86, 101-102; XVIII, 120.

10. *Private Papers*, XVIII, 171, 178, 184.

11. See Frank Brady, *Boswell's Political Career* (New Haven, 1965), p. 169, and Frederick A. Pottle, *The Literary Career of James Boswell, Esq.* (Oxford, 1929), p. 147.

12. *Private Papers*, XVIII, 271. This entry is dated 31 March 1794, not long before the journal ends and some thirteen months before Boswell's death.

13. *The Art of Biography in Eighteenth Century England* (Princeton, 1941), p. 345.

14. *Ibid.*, p. 346.

15. W. K. Wimsatt, Jr., in *The Prose Style of Samuel Johnson* (New Haven, 1941), pp. 135-138, argues against the notion that Johnson's friends formed such a "school."

16. Boswell praised Courtenay's "just and discriminative eulogy" on Johnson's Latin poems, and quoted it. See *Boswell's Life of Johnson*, ed. G. B. Hill, revised L. F. Powell (Oxford, 1934-1950), I, 62.

17. See *European Magazine*, IX (April 1786), 266; *Gentleman's Magazine*, LVI (May 1786), 415; *Monthly Review*, LXXV (September 1786), 229.

18. It should be noted that the attack on Courtenay in this poem is the mildest of the four. The famous caricaturist, Sayer, included Courtenay in a poetic attack on Mrs. Piozzi appended to his print, *Frontispiece to the 2nd Edition of Johnson's Letters*, published 7 April 1788. See James L. Clifford, *Hester Lynch Piozzi (Mrs. Thrale)* (Oxford, 1952), p. 329.

19. Boswell quoted Courtenay's compliment in *Life*, II, 268.

20. *Letters*, II, 444.

NOTES TO THE INTRODUCTION

1. See *DNB*.

2. For the information about Courtenay's election, I am indebted to Professor James M. Osborn of Yale University. Boswell gives no precise date for Courtenay's entry into the Club. His first reference to Courtenay's membership occurs in his journal entry of 19 January 1790. See *Private Papers of James Boswell*, ed. Geoffrey Scott and Frederick A. Pottle (Privately Printed, 1928-1934), XVIII, 22. See also Boswell's letter to Edmond Malone dated 16 December 1790, *Letters of James Boswell*, ed. C. B. Tinker (Oxford, 1924), II, 409-410. Courtenay and other intimates of Boswell were called "The Gang" by Philip Metcalfe. See *Private Papers*, XVII, 52, 55; XVIII, 15.

3. *Private Papers*, XVI, 106.

4. *Ibid.*, XVII, 80. For additional testimony to Courtenay's reputation as a wit, see *Thraliana*, ed. Katharine C. Balderston (Oxford, 1951), I, 486, and James Prior, *Life of Edmond Malone* (London, 1860), 287-288.

5. *Private Papers*, XVII, 86.

6. *Ibid.*, pp. 76-77.

7. *Ibid.*, XVI, 178. "M. C." is Mrs. Rudd.

8. See Boswell's letters to Malone, *Letters*, II, 405, 427, and *Private Papers*, XVIII, 100. Courtenay became alarmed over Boswell's deepening melancholy, as seen in this passage from his letter to Malone of 22 February 1791: "Poor Boswell is very low, & desperate & . . . melancholy mad, feels no spring, no pleasure in existence, & is so perceptibly altered for the worse that it is remarked everywhere. I try all I can to revivify him, but he [turns?] so tiresomely & tediously — for the same cursed trite commonplace topics, about death &c. — that we grow old, and when we are old, we are not young — that I despair of effecting a cure. Doctors Warren and Devaynes very kindly interest themselves about him, but you wd be of more service to him than anyone." Quoted from a MS at Yale University Library by James Osborn, "Edmond Malone and Dr. Johnson," *Johnson, Boswell and Their Circle: Essays Presented to Lawrence Fitzroy Powell in Honour of His Eighty-fourth Birthday* (Oxford, 1965), p. 16.

lines in all, mostly from Courtenay's commendatory verses. In view of the many published attacks on Johnson, Boswell must have appreciated Courtenay's sentiments all the more. Doubtless Courtenay's warm praise of the *Journal of a Tour to the Hebrides* also found favor with Boswell.[19] Perhaps Boswell's final and least partial judgment of the *Review* was expressed in his letter to James Abercrombie of Philadelphia dated 11 June 1792. He sent Abercrombie a copy of the poem, commenting that "though I except to several passages, you will find some very good writing."[20]

Courtenay's *Review,* together with several other little known *memorabilia* concerning Johnson, stimulated one of the most energetic and splenetic literary controversies of the late eighteenth century. In addition, the *Review* and pieces like it aroused a considerable amount of useful, if vitriolic, discussion about the art of biography.

University of Iowa

biographers and memorialists.[16] Furthermore, he employs footnotes skillfully. Though they impede the progress of the poem, they do support poetic statement with factual evidence and explain and amplify certain points made in the verses.

The clearest evidence for the care which Courtenay took with the *Review* can be found upon examination of his revisions. He made few substantial changes in the second edition, but the third edition contains important revisions. Courtenay added ten lines and five footnotes in the final version, and lightened some of the scorn in the first portion by substituting weaker phrases for stronger ones. He also enclosed lines seven through twenty in quotation marks to make it appear that the sentiment expressed therein was not his own, but a judgment he had heard elsewhere.

But the most significant revisions are concerned with organization. By transferring segments of certain verse paragraphs to others, he achieves a more unified portrait of Johnson. By means of such revision, he forms his general evaluation of Johnson's writing into one unit and his comments on individual works into another, where before they had been awkwardly interwoven.

Courtenay's *Review* did not go unnoticed at the time, though for obvious reasons it was given less attention by the reviewers than the more notorious Johnsoniana. Extracts from the poem were printed in several magazines. The reviewers were almost unanimous in damning the poem's inelegance, unevenness, and lack of harmony, but reserved praise for the sentiments and candor.[17] Chesterfield's apologist in William Hayley's *Two Dialogues; Containing a Comparative View of the Lives, Characters, and Writings of Philip, the Late Earl of Chesterfield, and Dr. Samuel Johnson* (1787) protested that Courtenay was too kind to Johnson. The severest indictment of the *Review* came from the anonymous author of *A Poetical Epistle from the Ghost of Dr. Johnson*, mentioned earlier, who charged Courtenay with poor taste and with belaboring the obvious by proving that Johnson was "not quite destitute of brains."[18]

The greatest champion of the *Review* was, of course, Boswell. The *Life* is sprinkled with quotations from the third edition, 118

The poem begins with disdain, but at line sixty-one reverses direction and becomes vigorously commendatory. Courtenay did not attempt to add fresh information about Johnson's life and career. Consequently, the unfavorable portion of the poem is a conventional catalog of Johnson's often publicized foibles and prejudices, just as the favorable section is in part a commonplace survey of his artistic achievement.

This contrast, as Stauffer remarks, renders Courtenay's praise more powerful.[14] More important, the play between scorn and praise reflects the ambivalence which colors contemporary accounts of Johnson. We are now accustomed to the notion of great art as the product of a flawed life. But in the eighteenth century, an age largely devoted to the idea of discreet biography which concealed or minimized the subject's weaknesses, a man like Johnson presented formidable problems to the biographer and his readers. Although Courtenay merely versified material which other writers had discussed in much more detail, his poem is important because it synthesizes the conflicting attitudes towards Johnson which prevailed immediately after his death. Courtenay, like many others, saw in Johnson a powerful mixture of great virtues and vices; and though he is not impartial, he effects, through his honesty, an admirable balance between Johnson's strengths and weaknesses. The final forty lines of the *Review* constitute one of the most balanced of all contemporary tributes to Johnson as a human being.

For the most part, the commendatory section of the poem is an unsystematic tracing of Johnson's moral and literary merits. Courtenay's rhapsodizing on the *Dictionary,* the *Rambler,* and the *Lives of the Poets* is conventional. Clearly, he admired the wide scope of Johnson's learning and his ability to communicate his knowledge of men and manners in his writings. But his admiration occasionally betrays him; for instance, in describing the "brilliant school" through which Johnson's influence was perpetuated, he overestimated the extent to which Reynolds, Malone, Burney, Jones, Goldsmith, Steevens, Hawkesworth, and Boswell were indebted to Johnson's writings.[15] Usually, however, he was on firmer ground. Courtenay was the only writer before Boswell to praise Johnson's Latin verse, a body of poetry virtually ignored by other contemporary lighten his published attacks on Mrs. Piozzi and helped make him aware of the merit of her edition of Johnson's correspondence, and advised him to cancel some questionable passages in the *Life* on William Gerard Hamilton. From time to time he also cautioned Boswell not to expect political preferment when he did not deserve it. It appears, too, that he took part in the prolonged deliberations over Johnson's monument in Westminster Abbey. Concerned that Boswell's drinking might impede his work on the *Life,* Courtenay made him promise to quit drinking from December 1790, to the following March, a promise which, as far as he was able, Boswell kept.[8]

Courtenay's high spirits and his ability to relieve Boswell's melancholy were all the more remarkable because Courtenay, with a wife and seven children to support, was poverty-stricken during most of this period. Boswell, lamenting the failure of the Whigs to provide financial assistance to one of the party's most active members, found Courtenay's "firmness of mind . . . amazing" under such difficulties.[9] No doubt Courtenay's resolve endeared him to Boswell, whose own financial and psychological problems were, of course, a great burden.

This is not to say that relations between the two men were always cordial. Courtenay was evidently a non-believer, and the two men often differed on religious matters. Boswell condemned Courtenay's "wild ravings" in favor of the French revolution, and once confessed his deep regret about quarreling with so close a friend on this subject.[10] They also differed on the question of slavery, and Boswell good-naturedly chided Courtenay and William Windham as abolitionists in his poem, *No Abolition of Slavery; or the Universal Empire of Love* (1791).[11] It is clear, too, that as Boswell's depression grew, Courtenay's power to brighten his spirits waned considerably. Their friendship, nevertheless, seems to have ended on a happy note, for Boswell's final mention of Courtenay in his journal includes the remark that with Courtenay he had spent a "good day."[12]

Courtenay's *Poetical Review,* characterized by Donald A. Stauffer as an embodiment of the "vice-and-virtue philosophy" in biography, was one of the most spirited pieces of Johnsoniana to appear.[13]

1788, by Sir Joshua Reynolds (Boswell seconded), and elected two weeks later, on 23 December, during the same meeting at which it was decided to erect a monument to Dr. Johnson in Westminster Abbey.[2]

If, then, Courtenay did not belong to the Johnson circle, he became, shortly after Johnson's death, a valued member of the Boswell circle. Courtenay must have met Boswell in the spring or early summer of 1785, about thirteen years after arriving in England from his native Ireland in the service of Viscount Townshend. Boswell's first reference to Courtenay occurs in his journal under 7 July 1785.[3] It is clear from this entry that he had met Courtenay earlier, but subsequent references indicate that the acquaintance was a fresh one.

From the start Boswell enjoyed Courtenay's company. In the first place, Boswell appreciated Courtenay's talent in conversation. Although he seldom recorded specimens of Courtenay's talk, Boswell was generous in his praise of his wit. "Courtenay's wit," he wrote, "sparkles more than almost any man's."[4] On 26 March 1788, Boswell described him as a "valuable addition" to a meeting of the Essex Head Club which he attended as Boswell's guest. "Indeed," Boswell continued, "his conversation is excellent; it has so much literature, wit, and at the same time manly sense, in it."[5] An example of his "manly sense" that "struck home" to Boswell was Courtenay's remark that had Johnson been born to three thousand pounds a year his melancholy would have been at greater leisure to torment him.[6]

But there was a greater reason for Courtenay's intimacy with Boswell. The period following Johnson's death was for Boswell a time of intense anxiety. By 1786 Courtenay and Edmond Malone had become Boswell's closest confidants. Boswell relished the long walks and the dinners he took with Courtenay. Throughout his journal he confessed to the therapeutic value of Courtenay's company; "I am," he admitted, "quite another Man with M. C., Malone, Courtenay."[7]

Moreover, Boswell often solicited Courtenay's advice in various crises. Courtenay, together with Malone, helped him out of scrapes with Alexander Tytler and Lord Macdonald, induced him to

INTRODUCTION

The eighteenth century was an age addicted to gossiping about its literary figures. This addiction was nowhere better demonstrated than by the countless reflections, sermons, poems, pamphlets, biographical sketches, and biographies about Samuel Johnson. The most productive phase of this activity commenced almost immediately after Johnson's death in December, 1784, and continued into the next century.

One item of Johnsoniana which seems to have been neglected, perhaps because Birkbeck Hill did not include it in his *Johnsonian Miscellanies,* is *A Poetical Review of the Literary and Moral Character of the Late Samuel Johnson, L.L.D., with Notes.* This poem of three hundred and four lines was written by John Courtenay (1741-1816). First published in the spring of 1786 by Charles Dilly, the poem went through three editions in the same year. Its popularity was determined less by Courtenay's poetic talent than by public interest in the Johnsoniana that flooded the market. Courtenay's literary output, though scanty, was diverse; he wrote light verse, character sketches, and essays, including two controversial pieces in support of the French Revolution.[1] It is apparent, however, that for him writing was hardly more than an avocation.

Despite his notoriety as a controversial member of Parliament, as a first-rate wit, and as an intimate friend of Boswell, Courtenay remains a shadowy figure. References to him occur often in the last volumes of Boswell's journal, but few of them are particularly revealing. Courtenay evidently never met Johnson; indeed, the anonymous author of *A Poetical Epistle from the Ghost of Dr. Johnson to His Four Friends: The Rev. Mr. Strahan. James Boswell, Esq. Mrs. Piozzi. J. Courtenay, Esq. M.P.* (1786) censures Courtenay for writing about a man whom he did not know. Although a member of the Literary Club, Courtenay did not join this group until four years after Johnson died. He was proposed on 9 December

GENERAL EDITORS

William E. Conway, *William Andrews Clark Memorial Library*
George Robert Guffey, *University of California, Los Angeles*
Maximillian E. Novak, *University of California, Los Angeles*

ASSOCIATE EDITOR

David S. Rodes, *University of California, Los Angeles*

ADVISORY EDITORS

Richard C. Boys, *University of Michigan*
James L. Clifford, *Columbia University*
Ralph Cohen, *University of Virginia*
Vinton A. Dearing, *University of California, Los Angeles*
Arthur Friedman, *University of Chicago*
Louis A. Landa, *Princeton University*
Earl Miner, *University of California, Los Angeles*
Samuel H. Monk, *University of Minnesota*
Everett T. Moore, *University of California, Los Angeles*
Lawrence Clark Powell, *William Andrews Clark Memorial Library*
James Sutherland, *University College, London*
H. T. Swedenberg, Jr., *University of California, Los Angeles*
Robert Vosper, *William Andrews Clark Memorial Library*

CORRESPONDING SECRETARY

Edna C. Davis, *William Andrews Clark Memorial Library*

EDITORIAL ASSISTANT

Mary Kerbret, *William Andrews Clark Memorial Library*